DADDY'S LITTLE HELPERS

by

Bil Keane

FAWCETT GOLD MEDAL • NEW YORK

DADDY'S LITTLE HELPERS

Published by special arrangement with The Register &
Tribune Syndicate, Inc., by Fawcett Gold Medal Books,
a unit of CBS Publications, the Consumer Publishing
Division of CBS Inc.

ISBN: 0-449-14384-8

Printed in the United States of America

First Fawcett Gold Medal printing: December 1980

10 9 8 7 6 5 4 3 2 1

"Breaker, breaker! How's it look over your shoulder, good buddy?"

"Hold still, Daddy, or I won't get you right."

"Why did you make that knothole?"

"Stay away from the car while Daddy shuts its mouth."

"Mommy's gonna wash her hair. She says we're all yours."

"I made the mistake of winning a game."

"Why is it named Jack?"

"Will you sit on the other end, Daddy, and make a hill?"

"...23, 24, 25, 26..." "Daddy said he wanted to take 40 winks. We're counting."

"The bus schedule is changed and it'll be here
twenty minutes earlier startin' today."

"Somebody let all the 'lectricity out of my bat-teries."

"I'm doin' real good in school this year. I'm the
third fastest runner in my class."

"Ask God to help you."
"I did but he's helpin' somebody else."

"He keeps waving that wand at them, but they won't disappear."

"I have $6.50 in my bank, Mommy. Now can we get a horse?"

"You can hang this one in the living room
'cause it took me two hours to color it."

"Mommy, will you fix Teddy's bionic eye?"

"If you don't put enough stamps on it the mail-
man will only take it part way."

"This is the three of valentines."

"My candy heart says 'kiss me.' Can I trade it for a different one?"

"I gained another inch on you, Daddy."

"Mommy! Dolly says I have dandruff!"

"This envelope has a little window for George Washington to look out of."

"The picture's flippin' and 'Sylvester and Tweety' are on."

"I'll bet the people who make pretzels are very good at tying their shoes."

"Is that your chemistry set?"

"When I get to be an angel I'm not going to play a harp. I'm going to play the drum."

"Were we good while Mrs. Bombeck was here, Mommy? Were we, Mommy? Were we good? Mommy?. . . ."

"How did they get the fly to sit still for his picture?"

"Billy tried to take my hula hoop away from me."

"I'd like to go through the express lane just once!"

"I was just testin' to see if the jello is done enough to eat."

"Why do they make beaters so hard to lick?"

"Watch me do a gymnastic."

"We'd better hang up now. This is costing money."

"Young man, you march into the bathroom and wash your hands!" "Hut! Two! Three! Four! . . ."

"Sorry, no passengers. This is a cargo run."

" . . . and bless me real hard 'cause I've got
that test tomorrow."

"No gravy for me. I like mine blank."

"I'll bet he can hug all his kids at once."

"The big hand caught the little hand."

"I think heaven is on television."

"I already got the cookies down 'cause I thought you'd say yes."

"If you get homesick for us while we're at
Grandma's, Mommy, you can phone us."

"Why do I have to be the one to carry the
FLOWERS for Grandma?"

". . . and these are full of toys to keep us busy, Grandma."

"Grandma, I'll sleep here on the couch if you
want me to."

"Do you use this little table and chairs very much when we're not here, Grandma?"

"These are FUNNY, Grandma! I like lookin' at pictures of Daddy when he was little."

"Billy! Jeffy! Stop that running and jumping!
Don't you know there are people living
downstairs?"

"We're walkin' on our tippy-toes, Grandma, so we don't bother the peoples downstairs."

"But, Grandma! We don't watch 'As the World Turns.' This is when we always watch 'Sesame Street!'"

"Grandma sure spends a lot of time talkin' to the maintenance man. I think maybe he's her boy friend."

"Mommy? . . . Guess who this is . . . no, wrong
. . . no . . . guess again . . . no . . . give up?
It's Billy! . . . Billy! . . . aw, Mommy,
you know Billy who . . . no. . . .
Your SON Billy! . . . Yeah! . . ."

"Thank you for a very nice time, Grandma!
We'll come visit you again — maybe
TOMORROW!"

"MMM! When I get to be President I'm gonna
put you in charge of cookies for
the whole country!"

"At Grandma's we got the choice of six different kinds of cereal in little boxes."

"We like the sermon part best. That's when Daddy gets to take PJ outside and Mommy passes us mints."

"Can I have approached egg like Grandma always has?"

"What kind of wax does Grandma use 'cause her floors are shinier than ours."

"Mommy has laryngitis. That means she's lost her sound."

"You can hardly see the street! I think a cloud fell down!"

"When we ask Grandma for a drink we get soda, but Mommy just gives us RAW WATER."

"Who NEEDS May flowers?"

"Billy! You forgot your books!"

"Robins must like baseball. They always come back when the season starts."

"Mommy, can you yell at Billy a little quieter?
We can't hear televison."

" 'Toddler' means you're too old to be a baby
and too young to be a little boy."

"Mommy, are you gonna take us to see the
Easter Bunny so we can tell him
what we want for Easter?"

"Mommy, do you remember where I hid the Easter card I made for you?"

"How come the Easter Bunny hides the eggs in the same places every year?"

"Watch him make a fist of himself."

"I didn't ask Billy HOW he did it — He was
phoning from the Principal's office to
say he'd split his pants."

"Mommies cook, talk on the phone, and hug you."

"But I took a bath LAST week!"

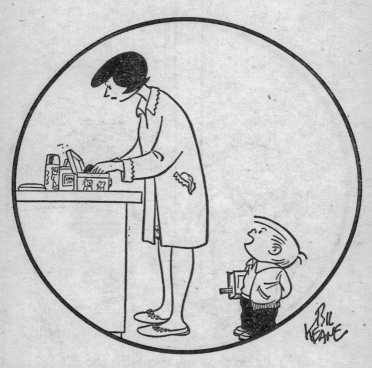

"L'eave a little room in my lunchbox, Mommy.
I'm taking my mouse for show and tell."

"PJ's on the new rug with food!"

"Hold onto the railing, Jeffy!"

"This cake I brought home from the party turned into a napkin full of crumbs."

"This is a neat vacation place! Can we stay
here for a YEAR?"

"We better keep PJ away from this railing
'cause he might fall through."

"Billy, you better stay in the shallow end."

"But the sun's up and WHO wants to spend
their whole vacation in BED?"

"But Sam doesn't even KNOW he's a dog!
He's one of the family!"

"Not so far out, Daddy, not so far out!"

"I hit the ocean!"

"Where can I ride my skateboard?"

"But I CAN'T go to the bathroom myself —
this isn't our house!"

"I made Prince Charming's castle and his garage."

"Every day God lets some of the water out so
there's room to play on the beach."

"This little kitchen is better than our big one at
home 'cause it saves you steps —
right, Mommy?"

"I wonder if they can do MY favorite — the belly flop."

"You'll never empty out the whole ocean your-self, PJ! Here — I'll help you!"

"Lift me up! Quick, Daddy, lift me UP! Here
comes a BIG one!"

"NO! NO!"

"Can't we wait t'see if it stops, Mommy?
Maybe it's just a SHOWER!"

"But why CAN'T we go down to the beach today? Nothin' would get wet but our BATHIN' SUITS!"

" . . . and this welcomed, much-needed rain
will continue along the coast for . . ."

"But I don't need a shower! I just came out of the OCEAN!"

"Dolly hit me on my SUNBURN!"

"Is it okay if I don't sit down? There's too
much SAND in the tub!"

"Clams leave their dishes all over the place!"

"MOMMY!"

"Somebody should clean the ring around this ocean."

"Stop laughing, Billy! I HAFTA walk like this
'cause my bathin' suit is full of SAND!"

"It's a sandcrab, Mommy! Can we keep him?"

"Hear that gull? He's yellin' at the fishies."

"What time do they turn off the waves?"

"Daddy, do I have much hair under my arms?"

"AGAIN? I thought the convention was all over!"

"Hi, there! I'm the castle inspector."

"I'm tellin'! It hasn't been an hour since you ate!"

"Wow! There's sure a lot of sand down here!"

"When the lifeguard blows his whistle does that mean somebody's drownin'?"

"Hurry up, Daddy, before the ocean erases it!"

"You've had Daddy long enough, Jeffy. Let somebody else have him for awhile!"

"Look at those words chasing the plane!"

"Wow! Look at the footprints! It must've been the ABOMIN'BLE SANDMAN!"

"Don't bother me! It's the last day of vacation
and I have 101 postcards to write!"

"Do we HAFTA leave? This place was just gettin' to feel like home."

"Goodby, ocean! 'Bye, beach! So long, gulls . . ."

"I can't sleep 'cause I can't hear the ocean."

"This water doesn't taste as good as the ocean."

"Got some room left in that hug, Mommy?"

Have Fun with the Family Circus

ANY CHILDREN?	14116	$1.50
DADDY'S LITTLE HELPERS	14384	$1.50
DOLLY HIT ME BACK!	14273	$1.50
GOOD MORNING SUNSHINE!	14356	$1.50
FOR THIS I WENT TO COLLEGE?	14069	$1.50
NOT ME!	14333	$1.50
I'M TAKING A NAP	14144	$1.50
LOOK WHO'S HERE	14207	$1.50
PEACE, MOMMY, PEACE	14145	$1.50
PEEKABOO! I LOVE YOU!	14174	$1.50
WANNA BE SMILED AT?	14118	$1.50
WHEN'S LATER, DADDY?	14124	$1.50
MINE	14056	$1.50
SMILE!	14172	$1.50
JEFFY'S LOOKIN' AT ME!	14096	$1.25
CAN I HAVE A COOKIE?	14155	$1.50
THE FAMILY CIRCUS	14068	$1.50
HELLO, GRANDMA?	14169	$1.50
I NEED A HUG	14147	$1.50
QUIET! MOMMY'S ASLEEP!	13930	$1.50

Buy them at your local bookstore or use this handy coupon for ordering.

COLUMBIA BOOK SERVICE (a CBS Publications Co.)
32275 Mally Road, P.O. Box FB, Madison Heights, MI 48071

Please send me the books I have checked above. Orders for less than 5 books must include 75¢ for the first book and 25¢ for each additional book to cover postage and handling. Orders for 5 books or more postage is FREE. Send check or money order only.

Cost $_____ Name_____

Sales tax*_____ Address_____

Postage_____ City_____

Total $_____ State_____Zip_____

*The government requires us to collect sales tax in all states except AK, DE, MT, NH and OR.

This offer expires 1 August 81   8067